100 Bundt and Tube Pan Cake Recipes

Tera L. Davis

TERA L. DAVIS

Copyright © 2013 Tera L. Davis

All rights reserved.

ISBN-13: 978-1490372723

CONTENTS

CAKES WITH FRUIT — 10

APRICOT PRESERVE CAKE — 10
BERRY BLUEBERRY CAKE — 12
APPLE ANNIE CAKE — 13
EASY STRAWBERRY CAKE — 14
BANANA WALNUT CAKE — 15
YUMMY STRAWBERRY CAKE — 16
TOASTED NUT APPLE CAKE — 18
CHERRY CAKE WITH PECANS — 19
APPLE NUT CAKE — 20
MANGO BANANA CAKE — 21
BANANA CRUNCH BUNDT CAKE — 22
APPLE PECAN CAKE — 23
TROPICAL ISLAND CAKE — 24
APPLE SWIRL CAKE — 26
LEMON AND CHEESE CAKE — 27
BANANA CHOCOLATE CHIP CAKE — 28
EASY PEASY CAKE — 29
RAW APPLE AND NUT CAKE — 30
PRUNE CAKE — 31
ANNIE APPLE CAKE — 33
CHERRY BANANA BUNDT CAKE — 34
BANANA AND RUM CAKE — 36
APRICOT NECTAR CAKE — 37
CAKE THAT DOESN'T LAST — 38
CALIFORNIA CITRUS CAKE — 39
ORANGE CAKE — 40
COCONUT CAKE — 41

CHOCOLATE CAKES — 43

TRIPLE CHOCOLATE CAKE — 43
CHOCOLATE MAYONNAISE CAKE — 44
MOIST CHOCOLATE CHIP CAKE — 45
SOUR CREAM CHOCOLATE CHIP CAKE — 46

PUMPKIN CHOCOLATE CHIP CAKE	47
CHOCOLATE COCONUT CAKE	48
BLACK CHOCOLATE CAKE	49
CHOCOLATE CAKE	50
AWESOME CHOCOLATE CAKE	51
ORANGE CHOCOLATE CAKE	52

COFFEE CAKES 54

COBBLESTONE COFFEE CAKE	54
RUM-FLAVORED COFFEE CAKE	55
STREUSEL COFFEE CAKE	56
NUTTY CINNAMON COFFEE CAKE	58
TP&L COFFEE CAKE	59

POUND CAKES 61

DELICIOUS POUND CAKE	61
APPLE POUND CAKE	62
LEMON POUND CAKE	63
COCONUT ISLAND POUND CAKE	64
EASY COCONUT POUND CAKE	65
COLD OVEN POUND CAKE	66
POUND CAKE WITH CHOCOLATE	67
POOR MAN POUND CAKE	68
POUND CAKE	69
KENTUCKY POUND CAKE	70
PINEAPPLE POUND CAKE	71

FRUIT CAKES 73

WHITE FRUIT CAKE	73
STIRRING FRUIT CAKE	74
ORANGE FRUIT CAKE	76
FESTIVE FRUIT CAKE	77

NUT CAKES 79

BLACK WALNUT CAKE	79
TEXAS PECAN CAKE	80
CHERRY AND WALNUT CAKE	81
WOODLAND NUT CAKE	82
GRANDMOTHER'S NUT CAKE	84
WATERGATE CAKE	85

MISCELLANEOUS CAKES 87

YOGURT CAKE	87
BUTTER CAKE	88
SO GOOD CAKE	89
KING YELLOW CAKE	90
ORANGE PUMPKIN CAKE	91
HERB BUBBLE RING	92
KAILUA CAKE	93
LEMON LIME CAKE	94
RICOTTA CAKE	95
HOLY COW CAKE	96
PECAN CARROT CAKE	97
SIMPLE BUTTER CAKE	98
FEATHER SPONGE CAKE	99
HOT MILK CAKE	100
SUNSHINE CAKE	101
THE WATERMELON CAKE	102
ZUCCHINI BUNDT CAKE	103
MARVELOUS MARBLE CAKE	104
ZESTY LIME CAKE	106
SIMPLE SOUTHERN CAKE	107
SO EASY DREAMSICLE CAKE	108

HOLIDAY CAKES 110

MOIST APPLE RING CAKE	110
EASY EGGNOG POUND CAKE	111
ORANGE PASSOVER NUT CAKE	112
MINCEMEAT CAKE	113
RUM AND PECAN CAKE	114

CHRISTMAS CAKE	115
THANKSGIVING PUMPKIN CAKE	116
SPICE AND PUMPKIN CAKE	117
CHRISTMAS CANDY CAKE	118
RUM EGGNOG BUNDT CAKE	119
YUMMY RUM CAKE	120
KAILUA CAKE	121
BREAKFAST BUNDT CAKE	122
MEXICAN BREAKFAST BUNDT	123

100 Bundt and Tube Pan Cake Recipes

Cakes are a thing of beauty, the centerpiece on a birthday table and the anticipated feeling that something lovely and sweet is coming your way. Holidays such as Christmas, Thanksgiving and Easter are full of homemade cakes that family and friends look forward to every year. The smell of a cake baking in the oven brings back fond memories for most of us and gives children the comforting feeling of home.

Here are 100 recipes for cakes baked in Bundt pans or tube pans. Bundt pans are tube pans; the main difference between the two, is that the Bundt pan has its own built-in design, whereas the tube pan has smooth sides. The Bundt cake has little need for decoration since its form is its decor. Bundt cakes are commonly served as is or just dusted with powdered sugar or with an easy to make powdered sugar glaze that is simply drizzled over a cooled cake. Modern Bundt pans have a non-stick surface and are great for creating beautiful cakes with no breakage.

Tube pans make for a taller and evenly baked cake. Cakes baked in a tube pan have a more dense surface area and are therefore easier to decorate with your favorite frosting, fruits, candies or whatever. You can find an array of shapes in tube pans, such as a star, heart, wreath and others. The recipes in this book that require a tube pan do not mention a certain shape, but you can certainly choose one of the above shapes for your cake as long as it is large enough to hold the cake batter.

Tips for non-stick baking:

1. When using a tube pan with a non-stick surface, it isn't necessary to spray or grease and flour the pan.

2. Unless otherwise specified, older tube pans and Bundt pans will usually need to be greased and dusted with flour; being sure to get into every nook and cranny.

3. Non-stick cooking spray containing flour works great and is easy to find at your grocery store's baking aisle.

4. When a cooked cake has pulled away from the sides of the pan, it's a good indication that it is ready to be turned out.

Cakes with Fruit

CAKES WITH FRUIT

APRICOT PRESERVE CAKE

1 cup margarine or butter

2 cups sugar

4 eggs

1 cup apricot preserves

1 teaspoon baking soda

1 cup buttermilk

3 cups flour

1 teaspoon cinnamon

1 cup pecans, chopped

8 ounces dried apricots, diced

Cream together the sugar and margarine. Add each egg one at a time, beating well. Add preserves and beat. Dissolve baking soda in buttermilk. Sift together the flour and cinnamon; mix into the creamed mixture alternating with the one cup of buttermilk. Stir in pecans and apricots.

Pour into a greased and flour dusted Bundt pan and bake in a preheated 325 degree F. oven for 1 hour and 15 minutes. Perform doneness test with toothpick. Cool only a few minutes before removing from pan.

BERRY BLUEBERRY CAKE

1 box yellow cake mix

1/2 cup applesauce

3 eggs, medium size

8 ounces lemon yogurt

3 cups fresh blueberries

2 tablespoons flour

1/4 cup pecans, chopped

1/4 cup sugar

1 teaspoon cinnamon

In a large bowl, mix together the yellow cake mix, applesauce, eggs and yogurt. Place blueberries and flour into a small bowl and toss until blueberries are well coated. Add 2 cups of cake batter and stir together well. Pour half of the cake batter into tube pan that has been greased and dusted with flour, then top with the blueberry batter.

Mix together the sugar, pecans and cinnamon in a small bowl, sprinkle over blueberry batter in tube pan. Top with the remaining cake batter. Bake in a preheated 350 degree F. oven for 1 hour. Let cake cool for 15 to 20 minutes. Invert cake onto rack. Serve with vanilla ice cream if desired.

APPLE ANNIE CAKE

2 eggs

2 cups sugar

1 1/4 cups oil

1 teaspoon salt

3 cups flour

1 teaspoon baking soda

1 teaspoon cinnamon

2 teaspoons vanilla extract

3 cups apples, coarsely chopped

1/2 cup pecans, chopped

Combine eggs, sugar, and oil, beat well; stir in salt, flour, baking soda, cinnamon, vanilla, apples, and nuts. Bake in a greased and flour dusted Bundt pan in a preheated 375 degree F. oven for 60 to 70 minutes.

EASY STRAWBERRY CAKE

1 angel food cake, small

3 small pkg. strawberry gelatin

3 cups boiling water

1 pkg. frozen strawberries, partially thawed

Whipped topping

Dissolve gelatin in boiling water. Add partially thawed strawberries. Pour into Bundt pan. Push angel food cake down into pan until mixture is absorbed and cake stays set. Serve with whipped topping if desired.

BANANA WALNUT CAKE

1 box cake mix, yellow

1 box cheesecake instant pudding, small

4 eggs

3/4 cup water

3/4 cup vegetable oil

1 teaspoon vanilla flavoring

1 teaspoon butter flavoring

1/2 cup walnuts, chopped

2 bananas, mashed

Using a large mixing bowl, mix together all ingredients for approximately 5 to 7 minutes. Pour in a greased and flour dusted Bundt pan. Bake in a preheated 350 degree F. oven for 35 to 45 minutes. Use a toothpick to perform doneness test.

YUMMY STRAWBERRY CAKE

3 tablespoons flour

1 box cake mix, white

1/2 cup water

1 box strawberry gelatin, 3 oz.

1/2 cup oil

4 eggs, medium size

1 cup strawberries, frozen

Thaw frozen strawberries and chop into small pieces; set aside. In a large bowl, mix together flour, cake mix, water and strawberry gelatin. Mix in oil and one egg at a time, beating mixture between each egg addition. Place strawberries into batter and beat for approximately 2 minutes. Pour the batter into a greased and flour dusted Bundt pan. Bake in a preheated 350 degree F. oven for 45 to 50 minutes. Insert toothpick for doneness test.

Frosting:

1/2 cup butter

10 ounces frozen strawberries, thawed

8 ounces cream cheese

5 to 6 cups powdered sugar

8 to 10 fresh strawberries

Soften butter and cream cheese and place in mixing bowl; add remainder of the frosting ingredients except for the fresh strawberries and mix well. Frost cooled cake. Remove stems from fresh strawberries and slice lengthwise; place on top of frosted cake.

TOASTED NUT APPLE CAKE

1 1/2 cups pecans, chopped

1/2 cup butter

1 1/2 cups vegetable oil

2 cups sugar

3 eggs

1/8 teaspoon table salt

1 1/4 teaspoon baking soda

1 teaspoon cinnamon

1 teaspoon nutmeg

1 tablespoon vanilla

2 cups flour

3 1/2 cups apples, diced

1 box powdered sugar, optional

On shallow pan or cookie sheet, toast pecans in 1/2 cup butter in 350 degree F. oven for 20 minutes; stir often. Cream oil and sugar, add all 3 eggs and beat well. Add salt, baking soda, spices and vanilla, beat again. Add flour one cup at a time, beating well after each addition. Cake batter will be very think. Stir in apples and nuts with a spoon. Pour batter into a tube pan that has been greased and dusted with flour. Bake 1 1/2 hours in a preheated 350 degrees F. oven. Sprinkle with powdered sugar if desired.

CHERRY CAKE WITH PECANS

2 cans cherry pie filling
1 or 2 cups pecans, chopped
1 box yellow cake mix
1 cup margarine, melted

Put pie filling in Bundt pan, sprinkle cake mix on top, then sprinkle with chopped nuts and pour melted margarine on top. Bake 1 hour in a 300 degree F. preheated oven.

APPLE NUT CAKE

8 to 10 apples

2 teaspoons cinnamon

2 1/3 cups sugar

1 cup vegetable oil

4 eggs, large

2 1/2 teaspoons vanilla flavoring

1 teaspoon salt

1 tablespoon baking powder

3 cups flour

1/3 cup orange juice

1 cup walnuts, chopped

Peel and cut apples into chunks. Sprinkle cinnamon and 1/3 cup sugar over apples and toss, set aside. Cream the remaining sugar, oil, eggs and vanilla. Sift or mix well the dry ingredients; add alternately to creamed mixture with orange juice. Stir in walnuts.

Spoon 1/2 of the batter into a greased and flour dusted Bundt pan. Place 1/2 of apple mixture on top (use juices that form also). Spoon on the rest of the batter. Place remaining apple mixture on top. Bake in a preheated 350 degree F. oven for 1 1/2 hours.

MANGO BANANA CAKE

2 teaspoons baking soda

1/2 teaspoon salt

2 cups flour

2 teaspoons ground cinnamon

3 eggs, beaten lightly

2/3 cup olive oil, ultra-light

2 tablespoons Kailua

1 very ripened banana, mashed

1 1/4 cups sugar

2 cups fresh mango, diced

1 teaspoon vanilla flavoring

1 cup walnuts, floured and roasted

Lightly oil Bundt pan and dust with a little sugar. Combine baking soda, salt, flour and cinnamon in a bowl; create a hole in the center of the mix. In a separate mixing bowl blend together the remaining ingredients and pour into the hole, mix well. Let batter stand for at least 20 minutes. Pour batter into the Bundt pan and cook in a preheated 350 degree F. oven for approximately 30 to 45 minutes.

BANANA CRUNCH BUNDT CAKE

1 pkg. frosting mix, coconut/pecan

1 cup rolled oats

5 tablespoons butter, softened

1 cup sour cream

2 ripe bananas, large

4 eggs

1 box yellow cake mix

Mix together the frosting mix, rolled oats and butter then set aside. Place the sour cream, bananas, eggs and cake mix into a large mixing bowl and blend together.

Pour 1/3 of the cake batter into a greased and flour dusted Bundt pan then pour 1/3 of the oat mixture on top. Repeat two more times. Bake in a preheated 350 degree F. oven for 1 hour. Insert toothpick for clean test. Let cake cool in pan for 15 minutes.

APPLE PECAN CAKE

1 cup salad oil

2 cups sugar

3 eggs

1 teaspoon vanilla

3 cups flour

1 1/4 teaspoons baking soda

1 teaspoon salt

1/2 teaspoon nutmeg

1 teaspoon cinnamon

1/2 teaspoon cloves

3 cups diced fresh apples

1 cup pecans

Combine oil, sugar, eggs and vanilla; mix well. Add flour, baking soda, salt and spices; blend. Then add diced apples and pecans. Bake in a greased and flour dusted Bundt pan in a preheated 350 degree F. oven for 1 hour or until done.

TROPICAL ISLAND CAKE

2 cups sugar

1 teaspoon baking soda

3 cups flour

1 teaspoon cinnamon

1 teaspoon salt

1 cup almonds, chopped

3 eggs

1 1/2 cups vegetable oil

2 cups bananas, chopped

1 teaspoon almond flavoring

1 can crushed pineapple, 8 oz.

Mix well the sugar, baking soda, flour, cinnamon and salt; stir in chopped almonds. Slightly beat the 3 eggs. Mix together the oil, bananas, almond flavoring and pineapple with juice. Add wet mixture to the dry ingredients; mix well, but do not beat.

Spoon cake batter into well-oiled ten inch tube pan. Bake cake in a preheated 325 degrees F. oven for 1 hr. and 20 minutes. Remove from oven; let cool for 10 to 15 minutes in pan. Turn cake out on wire rack and let cake cool before applying frosting.

Frosting:

8 ounces cream cheese, room temperature

1/2 cup butter, room temperature

1 lb. powdered sugar

1 tablespoon instant chocolate

In a large bowl cream together all the above. Frost the top and sides of cooled cake. Stores in refrigerator until ready to serve.

APPLE SWIRL CAKE

2 teaspoons cinnamon

4 tablespoons sugar

1 box cake mix, yellow

3 eggs

1 2/3 cups applesauce

Place cinnamon and sugar in a bowl and mix together. Generously grease Bundt pan and dust bottom and sides with 1 tablespoon of the cinnamon and sugar mixture; save remainder for cake.

Combine cake mix, eggs and applesauce until moistened, then beat as directed on cake box. Set aside 1 1/2 cups of cake batter. Slowly pour the remaining batter into the Bundt pan and dust with the remaining cinnamon and sugar mixture, top this with the 1 1/2 cups of batter that was set aside.

Cook cake in a preheated 350 degree F. oven for 35 to 45 minutes. Perform doneness test. Cake should cool in pan for approximately 15 minutes then turn out on to a cake dish. Put desired glaze on top.

LEMON AND CHEESE CAKE

1 box golden butter cake mix

3 eggs, large

1/4 cup butter, softened

3/4 cup apricot nectar

1/4 cup sugar

8 ounces cream cheese, room temp.

1/2 cup coconut, flaked

1 tablespoon lemon juice

Grease and dust a Bundt pan with flour. In a large mixing bowl, stir together cake mix, eggs, butter and apricot nectar. Beat with hand-held electric mixer as directed on cake mix box. Pour batter evenly into Bundt pan. For the filling, combine the remainder of ingredients in a small bowl beat until smooth and creamy. Spoon the filling over the batter in pan; do not let the filling touch the sides of the Bundt pan. Bake in a preheated 350 degree F. oven for 50 to 55 minutes. Cool in pan for 1 hour.

Glaze:

2 tablespoons lemon juice
2 tablespoons apricot nectar
2 cups powdered sugar

Mix together all 3 ingredients and using a spoon drizzle over cooled cake.

BANANA CHOCOLATE CHIP CAKE

4 cups flour

2 teaspoons baking soda

1 teaspoon salt

2 teaspoons baking powder

2 cups granulated sugar

1 cup soft margarine

4 eggs

1 cup milk

2 teaspoons vanilla flavoring

4 bananas, mashed

12 ounces chocolate chips

Grease and dust a Bundt pan with flour. Sift the flour, baking soda, salt and baking powder together and set aside. Cream sugar and soft margarine. Add each egg one at a time, beat mixture well after each egg addition. Add the dry ingredients, milk and vanilla. Fold in mashed bananas and chocolate chips. Pour cake batter into Bundt pan. Bake inside a preheated 350 degree F. oven for 50 to 60 minutes. Insert toothpick for doneness test. Let cake cool completely then turn out and dust with powder sugar.

EASY PEASY CAKE

3 cups flour

2 cups granulated sugar

1 teaspoon baking soda

1 teaspoon cinnamon

1 teaspoon salt

1 can pineapple crushed & drained 8 oz.

1 1/4 cups vegetable oil

1 1/2 teaspoons vanilla flavoring

3 eggs

1 1/3 cups pecans, chopped

Do not use mixer! Mix together dry ingredients and add pineapple, vegetable oil, vanilla extract and eggs. Mix until well blended. Blend in nuts. Pour cake batter into a greased tube pan and bake in preheated 350 degrees F. oven for 1 hour and 20 minutes.

RAW APPLE AND NUT CAKE

1 teaspoon baking soda

3 cups flour

1 teaspoon salt

2 cups sugar

3/4 cup vegetable oil

3 eggs

2 teaspoons vanilla flavoring

3 cups apples, chopped

1 cup pecans, chopped

Sift baking soda, flour and salt together. Mix sugar, oil, eggs, and vanilla. Blend together well and add pecans and chopped apples. Bake cake in a greased tube pan. Start in cold oven set at 375 degrees F. for 1 hour and 45 minutes or until done.

PRUNE CAKE

1 cup oil

1 1/2 cups sugar

3 eggs

1 teaspoon cinnamon

1 1/2 teaspoons baking soda

1 teaspoon salt

2 cups flour

1 teaspoon nutmeg

1 cup buttermilk

1 cup stewed prunes

1 cup walnuts, chopped

1 teaspoon vanilla flavoring

Combine oil and sugar, beating until smooth. Add eggs one at a time, beating well. In a separate bowl mix together dry ingredients. Then add dry ingredients to oil and sugar mixture alternately with milk. Fold in prunes, chopped nuts and vanilla. Pour into greased tube pan and bake in a preheated 350 degree F. oven for 45 to 55 minutes.

Topping:

1 cup sugar

1/2 teaspoon baking soda

1/2 cup buttermilk

1/4 cup butter

1 teaspoon corn syrup

1/2 teaspoon vanilla

Bring all ingredients to boil in large pan with cover, stir occasionally boiling 2-4 minutes. Pour over cake while it is still in pan. Let cool. Be careful when you turn this pan over. Cut around sides as cake breaks easily.

ANNIE APPLE CAKE

1/2 cup vegetable oil

2 cups sugar

2 medium eggs

1 teaspoon vanilla flavoring

3 cups flour

1 teaspoon baking soda

1 teaspoon cinnamon

1/2 teaspoon salt

3 cups apples, peeled & chopped

1 cup pecans, chopped

Cream oil, sugar, eggs and vanilla. Add flour, baking soda, cinnamon and salt. Mix and then add apples and pecans. Bake in a preheated 350 degree F. oven for 1 1/2 hours in a Bundt pan greased and dusted with flour.

CHERRY BANANA BUNDT CAKE

3 cups flour

1 teaspoon salt

1 1/2 teaspoons baking soda

2 cups granulated sugar

3/4 cup butter

4 eggs, beaten

2 teaspoons vanilla flavoring

1 3/4 cups ripe banana, mashed

3/4 cup sour cream

3/4 cup maraschino cherries, chopped

1 cup pecans, chopped

3/4 cup chocolate chips, semi-sweet

Grease and dust a Bundt pan with flour. Mix together the baking soda, flour and salt. In a large bowl, cream together sugar and butter, then beat in the eggs. Add vanilla, mashed bananas and sour cream, mix well. Stir in flour mixture. Fold into batter the cherries, pecans and chocolate chips. Pour cake batter into Bundt pan. Bake in a preheated 350 degree F. oven for 55 to 60 minutes. Let cake cool for 10 minutes. Turn cake onto a wire rack to continue cooling. Drizzle with chocolate glaze.

Chocolate Glaze:

1 cup powdered sugar

2 tablespoons milk

2 tablespoons corn syrup

1 envelope pre-melted chocolate

In a small bowl, beat together all of the ingredients and drizzle over Bundt cake.

BANANA AND RUM CAKE

2 cups self-rising flour

2 cups sugar

3 eggs, large

1 cup ripe banana, mashed

1/2 cup butter, unsalted

1/2 cup soy milk

1 tablespoon vanilla flavoring

1 teaspoon coconut flavoring

2 teaspoons banana flavoring

2 teaspoons rum or rum flavoring

Grease and dust a Bundt pan with flour. In a large mixing bowl, mix together all the ingredients and pour into Bundt pan. Bake in a preheated 350 degree F. oven for 45 to 55 minutes. Perform doneness test by inserting a toothpick.

APRICOT NECTAR CAKE

1 box yellow cake mix

1 box lemon gelatin

4 eggs

3 cups vegetable oil

1 teaspoon vanilla extract

1 teaspoon lemon extract

3 cups apricot nectar

Combine cake mix, gelatin, eggs, oil, vanilla, lemon extract, and apricot nectar. Mix thoroughly. Pour into a tube pan that has been greased and dusted with flour. Bake in a preheated 350 degree F. oven for one hour. Let cake cool. Punch holes in top of the cake with a toothpick.

FILLING:

1 cup sugar
3/4 cup apricot nectar
Dash vanilla

Bring filling ingredients to a boil. Cook 4 minutes. Pour over cake while cake is hot.

CAKE THAT DOESN'T LAST

2 cups sugar

3 cups flour

1 teaspoon salt

1 teaspoon baking soda

1 teaspoon cinnamon

3 eggs

1 can pineapple crushed & drained 8 oz.

1 cup pecans, chopped

1 cup coconut, optional

1 teaspoon vanilla

2 cups bananas, mashed

1 1/2 cups vegetable oil

In a large mixing bowl, mix together all dry ingredients; make a deep well in center of dry ingredients. Add eggs (beaten lightly with fork), pineapple, nuts, coconut, vanilla, bananas and vegetable oil. Do not beat, instead just stir. It will only take a few stirs to mix.

Pour into a Bundt pan that has been greased and dusted with flour. Bake in a preheated 350 degree F. oven for 65 to 70 minutes. Cool 1 hour before removing from pan. May decrease bananas and add more pineapple if desired. Ice with cream cheese frosting or ice with 1 cup powdered sugar mixed with 2 tablespoons pineapple juice.

CALIFORNIA CITRUS CAKE

4 eggs

1 box yellow cake mix

3/4 cup water

1/2 cup buttery flavored oil

1 pkg. instant pudding, lemon

Grease a 10 inch tube pan then dust with flour. Beat the four eggs; add cake mix, water, oil and pudding. Beat for approximately ten minutes. Pour cake batter into pan. Bake in a preheated 350 degrees F. oven for 50 minutes. Cool in pan. When cake has completely cooled, remove from pan; put on plate.

Glaze:

1/3 cup orange juice
2 cups sugar, powdered
2 tablespoons grated orange rind
Fresh orange slices

Combine juice and sugar and heat until boiling; stir in orange rind. Cool. When glaze has cooled, drizzle over cake. Use orange slices for garnishment.

ORANGE CAKE

3 eggs, separated

1 cup sugar

1 cup flour

2 teaspoons baking powder

1/2 cup orange juice grated orange rind

1 1/2 teaspoons vanilla

In small bowl, whip egg whites till very stiff. In large bowl, beat everything else together very thoroughly for 3 minutes, until smooth. Fold egg whites carefully into batter; pour mixture into greased tube pan.

Bake in a preheated 350 degree F. oven for 30 minutes. Let cake cool in pan 10 minutes. Cake is very light and fluffy. Can be served plain, with powdered sugar frosting, or with ice cream and mandarin oranges.

COCONUT CAKE

5 eggs, medium sized

2 cups granulated sugar

1 cup vegetable oil

1/2 cup milk, whole

2 cups flour

1 1/2 teaspoons baking powder

1/2 teaspoon salt

1 teaspoon vanilla flavoring

1 teaspoon coconut flavoring

3/4 cup coconut, flaked

Beat eggs and sugar. Add oil and beat. In a separate mixing bowl, mix together dry ingredients. Alternate adding milk and dry ingredients to sugar mixture; beating after each addition. Add vanilla extract, coconut extract, and flaked coconut. Mix together. Pour into a tube pan that has been greased and dusted with flour. Bake in a preheated 350 degrees F. oven for 1 hour.

Sauce:

1 cup sugar
1/4 cup margarine
1/2 cup water
1/2 teaspoon coconut extract
In a sauce pan, mix together sugar, water, margarine and coconut extract; boil 1 minute. Pour over warm cake in tube pan. Let cool in pan.

Chocolate Cakes

CHOCOLATE CAKES

TRIPLE CHOCOLATE CAKE

1 box cake mix, chocolate

1 pkg. chocolate pudding & pie filling

2 cups milk

2 eggs

1 pkg. chocolate chips, 12 oz.

Prepare pudding according to the directions on the package. While pudding cools, combine cake mix, milk and eggs, by hand, for one minute or until crumbly. Blend in warm pudding. Fold in chips.

Bake in a preheated 350 degree F. oven for 45 to 55 minutes in greased and flour dusted Bundt pan.

CHOCOLATE MAYONNAISE CAKE

1/4 cup cocoa powder

1 cup real mayonnaise

2 cups flour

1 cup sugar

2 teaspoons baking soda

1 cup water, warm

1 teaspoon vanilla flavoring

Place all the above ingredients into a large mixing bowl and mix just long enough to blend together. Pour batter into a greased Bundt pan and bake in a pre-heated 375 degree F. oven for 40 minutes. Cake is very moist.

MOIST CHOCOLATE CHIP CAKE

1 box butter cake mix

1 pkg. vanilla instant pudding mix

3/4 cup oil

4 eggs, one at a time

1/2 pint sour cream

1 teaspoon vanilla

1 pkg. chocolate chips, 6 oz.

1 1/2 cups chocolate syrup

Mix all ingredients except chocolate chips and syrup. Beat until smooth and creamy. Mixture will be stiff. Divide batter into two equal parts. To one part, add chips and syrup. Put half of yellow batter into a Bundt pan that has been greased and dusted with flour. Add chocolate mixture, add the remaining yellow batter. Swirl with knife. Bake 50-60 minutes in a preheated 350 degrees F. oven. Can be glazed, frosted or served plain.

SOUR CREAM CHOCOLATE CHIP CAKE

1 box yellow cake mix

8 ounces sour cream

3/4 cup water

6 ounces milk chocolate chips

1 pkg. instant milk chocolate pudding mix, 4.5 oz.

3/4 cup oil

3 eggs

Mix all ingredients except chips. Beat 4 minutes. Fold in chips. Bake in a preheated 350 degree F oven for 55 minutes in a large greased and floured Bundt pan.

PUMPKIN CHOCOLATE CHIP CAKE

12 ounces chocolate chips

3 cups flour

2 cups sugar

1 cup oil

4 eggs

1 can pumpkin, 16 oz.

3 tablespoons cinnamon

2 teaspoons baking soda

2 teaspoons baking powder

1 teaspoon salt

Mix all ingredients together well. Pour into greased and flour-dusted Bundt pan. Bake in a preheated 350 degrees F. oven for 1 hour and 20 minutes.

CHOCOLATE COCONUT CAKE

1 box yellow cake mix

1 box instant chocolate pudding

8 ounces sour cream

3/4 cup water or buttermilk

3/4 cup oil

4 eggs

1/4 cup sugar

7 ounces flaked coconut

1 small pkg. milk chocolate chips

1 1/2 cups pecans, chopped

Mix first seven ingredients. Fold in pecans, coconut and chocolate chips. Bake in a greased and flour dusted Bundt pan in a preheated 350 degree F. oven for 1 hour.

BLACK CHOCOLATE CAKE

2 cups sugar

2 cups flour

1 teaspoon baking powder

3/4 cup cocoa

2 teaspoons baking soda

2 eggs

1/2 cup vegetable oil

1 cup milk

1 cup coffee

2 eggs

1 teaspoon vanilla

In a large mixing bowl mix together the first five ingredients. Add remainder of ingredients and mix well. Bake inside a greased and flour dusted tube pan in a 350 degrees F. preheated oven for 45 minutes.

CHOCOLATE CAKE

2 cups of flour

1/2 cup shortening

2 cups of sugar

3/4 cup water

1 teaspoon baking soda

3/4 cup buttermilk

1 teaspoon vanilla

1 teaspoon salt

1/2 teaspoon baking powder

2 eggs

4 ounces unsweetened chocolate

Melt chocolate and let cool. Beat all the above ingredients on low speed for 30 seconds, scraping bowl constantly. Beat at high speed for three minutes, scrap bowl now and then.

Pour into a greased and flour dusted Bundt pan. Bake in a preheated 350 degree F. oven for 50 to 55 minutes. Perform doneness test with toothpick. Let cake cool for ten minutes and turn out onto wire rack and cool completely. Frost.

AWESOME CHOCOLATE CAKE

1 pkg. instant chocolate pudding, 4 serving size

1 pkg. chocolate chips (semi-sweet), 6 oz.

3/4 cup pecans or walnuts, chopped

1 box cake mix, chocolate

4 eggs

8 ounces sour cream

Coat the nuts and chocolate chips in a tablespoon of the dry cake mix. Beat the rest of the ingredients together for three minutes then fold in the coated chips and pecans.

Pour batter into a greased and flour dusted Bundt pan and bake in a preheated 350 degree F. oven for 50 minutes. Perform doneness test with toothpick.

ORANGE CHOCOLATE CAKE

1 egg

3/4 cup sugar

1/2 cup buttermilk

2 teaspoons very ripe banana, mashed

1 teaspoon orange peel, finely grated

2 1/2 tablespoons orange juice, fresh

1 teaspoon vanilla

1 cup flour, self-rising

1 teaspoon baking soda

1/2 cup chocolate chips, tiny semi-sweet

Cocoa powder and orange peel for garnish

Beat egg 2 minutes on medium speed, gradually add sugar. Add all ingredients except for the cocoa powder and orange peel and mix gently.

Pour batter into a greased and flour dusted Bundt pan and bake in a preheated 350 degree F. oven for 30 minutes or until it passes the toothpick test. Cool before removing from pan and garnish with cocoa powder and orange zest.

Coffee Cakes

COFFEE CAKES

COBBLESTONE COFFEE CAKE

2 cans biscuits cut into quarters

1/2 cup butter or margarine

1 cup brown sugar

1 teaspoon cinnamon

1 cup pecans, chopped

Mix butter, sugar, and cinnamon together. Line bottom of a Bundt pan with 1 can of cut-up biscuits. Pour 1/2 of butter mixture over biscuits. Put other can of biscuits on top. Pour remaining butter over top. Add nuts on top if desired. Bake in a preheated 375 degree F. oven for about 30 minutes or until crispy brown.

RUM-FLAVORED COFFEE CAKE

1 box cake mix, yellow

1 pkg. instant pudding, 3 3/4 oz.

4 eggs

1/2 cup oil, scant

8 ounces sour cream

1/3 - 1 ounce rum flavoring

Sugar and cinnamon for sprinkling

Put all ingredients in bowl and stir well. It is a stiff batter. Grease Bundt pan with margarine. Sprinkle with cinnamon and sugar. Pour mixture into pan. Sprinkle cinnamon and sugar on top. Bake in a preheated 350 degree F. oven for 45 - 50 minutes. Let cake cool before turning out.

STREUSEL COFFEE CAKE

1 cup graham crackers, finely crushed

1/2 cup packed brown sugar

1/2 cup pecans, chopped

1 teaspoon cinnamon

1/3 cup butter, melted

2 cups sugar

1/2 cup real butter, softened

4 eggs

1 cup milk

4 teaspoons baking powder

4 cups flour

1 teaspoon salt

1/2 jar ready-to-use mincemeat, 28 oz.

2 teaspoons grated orange peel

Grease tube pan (10x4 inches). Mix cracker crumbs, brown sugar, nuts, cinnamon and 1/3 cup melted butter in bowl with fork, set mixture aside. In a large bowl, beat together the white sugar and 1/2 cup softened butter on medium speed setting until fluffy and light. Beat in eggs, one egg at a time, until smooth. Add milk.

Beat in baking powder, flour and salt on low speed. Stir in mincemeat and orange peel. Spread half of the cake batter inside tube pan; dust with half of the reserved crumbly mixture.

Carefully spread remaining batter over crumbly in pan; dust with remaining crumbly mixture. Press lightly into batter. Bake in a preheated 350 degree F. oven for 70 minutes. Perform doneness test with toothpick. Cool 10 minutes; remove from pan.

NUTTY CINNAMON COFFEE CAKE

1 box yellow cake mix

1/2 cup oil

1 box instant vanilla pudding mix, small

4 beaten eggs, medium size

1 teaspoon vanilla

1 teaspoon butter

3/4 cup water

2 teaspoons ground cinnamon

1/4 cup sugar

1/4 cup pecans, chopped

Place cake mix, oil, pudding mix, eggs, vanilla, butter and water into a large bowl. Combine with an electric hand mixer on medium setting. In a small bowl, mix together cinnamon, sugar and pecans.

Place a small portion of the cinnamon mixture into the bottom of a well-greased Bundt pan, sprinkle evenly. Layer cake batter and cinnamon mixture until both are all gone. Bake in a preheated 350 degree F. oven for 50 to 60 minutes.

TP&L COFFEE CAKE

Frozen yeast rolls

1 cup brown sugar

1 teaspoon cinnamon

Butterscotch pudding (not instant)

1/2 cup pecans, chopped

1/2 cup butter, melted

Grease tube pan. Place frozen yeast rolls around tube pan evenly. On top of rolls sprinkle cinnamon, brown sugar, pudding and pecans. Pour melted butter over all. Allow to rise. Bake in a preheated 350 degrees F. oven for 30 minutes. Turn onto plate and serve.

I will do this at night before I go to bed, and it is ready to pop in the oven the next morning.

Pound Cakes

POUND CAKES

DELICIOUS POUND CAKE

1 pkg. cream cheese, 8 oz.

1 1/2 cups butter, softened

3 cups sugar

6 eggs, large

1 teaspoon vanilla

1 teaspoon almond extract

3 cups flour

Blend together the cream cheese and butter, combining the 3 cups sugar with hand-held electric mixer. Add each egg, one at a time, and continue to blend. Mix in almond and vanilla flavorings and flour; beat until batter is light and smooth.

Pour cake batter into a ten inch tube pan that has been greased and dusted with flour. Bake in oven that has been preheated to 325 degree F. for 1 1/2 hours or until cake is golden and tests done with toothpick test, about 2 hours.

APPLE POUND CAKE

2 cups granulated sugar

1 1/4 cups vegetable oil

3 eggs, large

3 cups flour

1 teaspoon baking soda

1 teaspoon salt

1 1/2 teaspoons vanilla

3 cups diced firm apple

3/4 cup flaked coconut

1 cup walnuts, chopped

Mix together the sugar and oil; add eggs and mix in the flour, salt and baking soda. Add to oil mixture. Stir in the vanilla flavoring, apples, coconut, and walnuts; mix well.

Spoon cake batter into a 9-inch tube pan that has been coated with oil. Bake in oven preheated to 325 degrees F. for one hour and twenty minutes or until cake tests done.

LEMON POUND CAKE

1 box yellow cake mix

1 pkg. lemon instant pudding

4 eggs

1/4 cup oil

1 1/4 cups water

1/2 teaspoon lemon extract

Combine all ingredients in large mixer bowl. Blend together then beat on medium speed setting with a hand-held electric mixer for four minutes.

Pour into a Bundt pan that has been greased and dusted with flour. Bake cake for 35 to 45 minutes in a preheated 350 degree oven. Test for doneness with toothpick. Cool 15 minutes and remove.

COCONUT ISLAND POUND CAKE

1 cup butter

3 cups granulated sugar

2/3 cup shortening

5 eggs, large

3 cups flour

1 teaspoon baking powder

1 cup milk

2 teaspoons coconut flavoring

1 1/2 cups coconut, flaked

Cream together the butter, granulated sugar and shortening. Add each of the eggs one at a time, beating well after each egg is added. Mix the baking powder and flour together. Alternate adding the flour and milk to the egg mixture. Beat well; stir in coconut flavoring and coconut.

Pour cake batter into greased and flour dusted tube pan. Bake cake for one hour and thirty minutes in a preheated 300 degree F. oven.

EASY COCONUT POUND CAKE

3 cups sugar

1/2 cup butter

6 eggs, large

3 cups flour

1/4 teaspoon salt

1/4 teaspoon baking soda

1 cup sour cream

1 teaspoon vanilla

6 ounces frozen coconut

Have all ingredients at room temperature. Preheat oven. Grease and dust a tube pan with flour. Cream well the sugar and butter. Add each egg one by one, and beat well after each addition. Add flour, salt, baking soda, sour cream and vanilla. Beat well.

Stir in the coconut, being careful to distribute it evenly. Pour into pan and bake in a preheated 350 degrees F. oven for one hour and fifteen minutes. This freezes beautifully; in fact, is even better after being frozen.

COLD OVEN POUND CAKE

1 cup butter

2 1/4 cups sugar

3 teaspoons baking powder

2/3 cup milk

2 teaspoons vanilla

1/2 cup margarine

3 cups flour

1/2 teaspoon salt

6 eggs

Put all ingredients in bowl and beat for 20 minutes. Turn into 10" tube pan that has been greased and dusted with flour, place in a cold oven, then turn oven to 350 degrees F., bake for 1 hour and 30 minutes.

POUND CAKE WITH CHOCOLATE

1/2 cup soft margarine

3 cups sugar

1/2 cup, and 1 tablespoon shortening

5 eggs

1/4 teaspoon salt

1/2 cup cocoa

1/2 teaspoon baking powder

3 cups flour

1 teaspoon vanilla flavoring

1 1/4 cups whole milk

1 box powdered sugar – for topping only

Cream together margarine, sugar and shortening, mixing well. Add the eggs one at a time and blend well after each one. Sift dry ingredients together and add alternately with vanilla flavoring and milk.

Pour cake batter into a Bundt pan that has been greased and dusted with flour. Bake 1 and 1/2 hours in a preheated 325 degrees F. oven. Sprinkle with powdered sugar after removing from pan. Especially good served with vanilla ice cream.

POOR MAN POUND CAKE

2 1/2 cups butter

3 cups sugar

5 eggs

1/2 teaspoon salt

3 cups flour

1 cup milk

1 tablespoon vanilla extract

1 tablespoon lemon extract

Cream butter well. Add the sugar a little at a time creaming well. Add the eggs one at a time, beating well. Sift flour with salt, add to the butter mixture alternately with milk, beat well. Mix in extract flavoring.

Put in a greased tube pan in cold oven. Bake in a preheated 325 degrees F. oven for 1 hour and 45 minutes.

POUND CAKE

1 box cake mix, yellow butter

1/2 cup buttery oil

1 cup sugar

6 eggs

1 cup sour cream

Mix all together and beat for 2 minutes. Pour into Bundt pan that's been greased and dusted with flour. Bake in a preheated 325 degree F. oven for about 1 hour. The ingredients listed should be used without substitution.

KENTUCKY POUND CAKE

1/2 cup oil

2 cups sugar

2 1/2 cups self-rising flour

1 can crushed pineapple, small

1 teaspoon cinnamon

4 egg whites, beaten until stiff

1 cup chopped pecans

Cream oil and sugar. Add flour with cinnamon, then pineapple. Fold in egg whites. Add pecans. Bake in tube pan that has been greased and dusted with flour. Bake in a preheated 350 degrees F. oven for 1 hour.

PINEAPPLE POUND CAKE

3 cups sugar

2 cups shortening

8 eggs, large

3 cups cake flour

1 small can crushed pineapple, drained (reserve juice)

2 teaspoons butter

2 teaspoons vanilla extract

Cream sugar and shortening well; add the eggs, 3 at a time. Add flour gradually. Add pineapple butter and vanilla, mixing well. Spoon batter into 10 inch tube pan that's been greased and dusted with flour. Bake in a preheated 275 degrees F. oven for 1 1/2 hours or until done. Glaze cake while hot.

Glaze:

1/2 box powdered sugar
Reserved pineapple juice
2 tablespoons butter, softened

Cream butter; add powdered sugar and pineapple juice, mixing well. Drizzle over cake.

Fruit Cakes

FRUIT CAKES

WHITE FRUIT CAKE

2 teaspoons baking powder

3 cups flour

1 cup butter

2 cups sugar

4 eggs, separated

2 cups milk

1/2 pound candied cherries

2 rings pineapple

1/4 pound flaked coconut

1 pound white raisins

1 pound pecans

Mix together flour and baking powder. Cream the sugar and butter; mix in egg yolks, milk, and flour mixture. Add cherries, pineapple, and coconut, mix well, then add raisins and nuts to batter. Beat egg whites and fold in last. Bake in lined angel food pan, for about 1 1/4 hours in a preheated 325 degrees F. oven. Test for doneness.

STIRRING FRUIT CAKE

1 lb. candied red cherries

1/2 lb. candied white pineapple

1/2 lb. candied green pineapple

1/4 lb. raisins or dates

3 pints pecans, chopped

1 cup sugar

1/2 lb. butter

4 large eggs

1 cup self-rising flour

2 teaspoons vanilla flavoring

2 teaspoons cake spice

2 teaspoons almond flavoring

Chop fruits coarsely, mix in pecans and set aside. Mix remainder of ingredients and pour over fruits and nuts; mix together thoroughly.

Grease a heavy pan or Dutch oven which can be put in the oven. Pour the cake in and bake in a preheated 375 degree F. oven for 15 minutes, then stir it well. When the cake has baked for 45 minutes, pack it in a tube pan which has been greased and lined with waxed paper. Bake for 15 minutes. Turn out on tin foil and wrap tightly.

This cake freezes well. (Be sure to pack the cake very well when you put it in the tube pan. I use the bottom of a glass, dipped in warm water, to pack with.

ORANGE FRUIT CAKE

2 oranges, rind and juice

2 cups raisins

3 cups pecans

1 cup butter, softened

2 cups sugar, divided

4 eggs

4 cups flour

2 teaspoons baking soda

1 teaspoon salt

1 1/3 cups sour milk*

2 teaspoons vanilla

Put orange rinds, raisins, and pecans through food grinder. Cream butter and 1 cup sugar well. Add eggs to butter mixture and beat until fluffy. Sift flour, baking soda, and salt together. Add flour mixture to butter mixture alternately with sour milk. Mix well and fold in fruit and nuts. Add vanilla. Turn batter into a tube pan that has been greased and dusted with flour. Bake 1 1/2 hours in 325 degree F. oven. Combine orange juice and 1 cup sugar. Stir several times while cake is cooking. Pour juice mixture over hot cake and let remain in tube pan until all juice is absorbed and partially cooled.

*To make sour milk, place 5 teaspoons vinegar in measuring cup and add enough milk to measure 1 1/3 cups.

FESTIVE FRUIT CAKE

1 box spice cake mix

1 can tomato soup

1/2 cup water

2 eggs

2 cups candied fruit, chopped

1 cup pecans, chopped

1 cup dates, chopped

In large bowl combine cake mix, soup, water and eggs. Beat as directed on package. After mixing, fold in fruit and pecans. Pour into a Bundt pan that has been greased and dusted with flour. Bake in a preheated 350 degree F. oven for 80 minutes. Cool 40 minutes; remove from pan. If desired glaze with warm corn syrup; decorate with candied fruits.

Nut Cakes

NUT CAKES

BLACK WALNUT CAKE

9 egg whites (no yolks)

2 cups butter, softened

2 cups sugar

2 1/2 teaspoons vanilla flavoring

4 cups flour

2 teaspoons baking powder

2 cups walnuts, chopped

Beat whites stiff. Mix butter and sugar together, add vanilla. Mix baking powder and flour together. Mix all ingredients. Pour into a well-greased tube pan and bake in a preheated 250 degree F. oven for 2 1/2 to 3 hours.

TEXAS PECAN CAKE

2 cups sugar

3/4 cup oil

1 teaspoon baking soda

2 cups flour

1 teaspoon salt

1 teaspoon ground cloves

1 teaspoon nutmeg

1 teaspoon allspice

2 teaspoons cinnamon

3 eggs

1 cup buttermilk

1 cup dates, chopped

2 cups pecans, chopped

Grease Bundt pan then dust with flour. Cream the sugar and oil with electric mixer. Sift all dry ingredients together. Stir in eggs, then alternate flour mixture with buttermilk. Mix in dates and nuts. Bake in a preheated 250 degree F. oven for 2 hours or until inserted toothpick comes out clean. Let cool.

CHERRY AND WALNUT CAKE

1 teaspoon baking soda

3 tablespoons sour cream

1 cup sugar

1/2 teaspoon salt

3/4 cup shortening

3 eggs

1/2 teaspoon salt

1 1/2 cups canned cherries, drained

1 cup walnuts, chopped

2 cups flour

Dissolve baking soda in sour cream and set aside. Place the sugar, salt and shortening in a large mixing bowl and cream together. Add the sour cream mixture and the remainder of the ingredients, blend well.

Pour batter into a Bundt pan that's has been greased and dusted with flour. Bake in a preheated 350 degree F. oven for 1 hour.

WOODLAND NUT CAKE

2 1/4 cups cake flour

1 3/4 cups sugar

2 teaspoons baking powder

1 1/2 teaspoons salt

1 cup shortening

3/4 cup milk

3 eggs, whole

1 egg yolk

1 teaspoon orange extract

1 teaspoon almond extract

1 cup nuts, chopped

Mix well the dry ingredients and place in a large mixing bowl. Make a center hole in the flour-sugar mixture and add the shortening, milk and one egg yolk in the center hole. Beat for two minutes. Add remaining eggs, flavorings and nuts. Beat well. Pour batter into a well-greased tube pan. Bake in a preheated 350 degrees F. oven for 1 hour.

Frosting:

3 teaspoons butter
1/4 teaspoon almond extract
4 tablespoons hot cream
2 1/2 cups powdered sugar

1 teaspoon vanilla
1 tablespoon orange rind, granted, or orange bits

Cream the butter. Add sugar, hot cream and flavorings. Spread on cooled nut cake.

GRANDMOTHER'S NUT CAKE

1 cup butter

2 cups sugar

5 eggs, separated

1 teaspoon vanilla

4 cups flour

1 1/2 teaspoons baking powder

1/2 teaspoon salt

4 cups pecans, chopped

1 1/2 lbs. seedless raisins

Cream butter and sugar. Add beaten egg yolks and vanilla. In another bowl mix dry ingredients together. Coat nuts and raisins with 1 cup of dry ingredients. Add remaining flour mixture alternately with beaten egg whites to creamed mixture. Add nuts and raisins. (I use my hands at this point, because the mixture is so very heavy.)

Bake inside a greased tube pan in a preheated 275 degrees F. oven for about three hours. Cool completely before taking out of pan. I use an angel food pan that comes apart, as this makes taking it out much easier.

WATERGATE CAKE

2 cups self-rising flour

1 1/2 cups sugar

1/4 cup powdered milk

1 small box pistachio instant pudding and pie filling

3 eggs

1 cup vegetable oil

1 cup club baking soda

1/2 cup pecans, chopped

Grease a Bundt pan and dust with flour. Mix together all the above ingredients with hand held mixer for 3 to 4 minutes. Pour batter in Bundt pan and bake in a preheated 350 degree F. oven for 30 to 40 minutes. Once cake has cooled, dust with powdered sugar.

Misc. Cakes

MISCELLANEOUS CAKES

YOGURT CAKE

1 box cake mix, white

1 small carton yogurt, any flavor

1 small box gelatin (same flavor as yogurt)

3/4 cup oil

4 eggs

In a large mixing bowl, add all ingredients (except for the eggs). Mix with a hand-held electric mixer on low speed. Add each egg one egg at a time and beat with electric mixer at medium speed.

Pour in Bundt pan that has been greased and dusted with flour. Bake in a preheated 300 degrees F. oven for 50 minutes to 1 hour.

BUTTER CAKE

1/2 cup soft margarine

1 cup soft butter

2 1/2 cups granulated sugar

7 eggs, large

3 cups flour

2 teaspoons vanilla or lemon extract

Cream the butter, margarine and sugar until fluffy and light. Add each egg one egg at a time. Beat well. Add flour and vanilla to creamed mixture.

Pour batter into a 10 inch tube pan or Bundt pan that has been greased and dusted with flour. Bake 1 hour and 20 minutes in a preheated 275 degrees F. oven, then 10 minutes at 300 degrees F. Cool 10 minutes; remove from pan.

SO GOOD CAKE

1 cup oil

2 cups sugar

2 eggs

1 teaspoon baking soda

2 teaspoons baking powder

1 teaspoon cinnamon

1 1/2 cups flour

1 teaspoon salt

1 teaspoon vanilla

3 cups diced apple

1 cup nuts

1/2 cup flaked coconut

1 pkg. butterscotch chips

Put oil in large bowl, add sugar and eggs. Sift dry ingredients together and add to sugar mixture. Beat until smooth. (Batter will be extremely thick.) Add vanilla, fold in apples, nuts and coconut. Put in greased and floured angel food cake pan. Sprinkle butterscotch chips over top of cake.

Pour batter into a Bundt pan that has been greased and dusted with flour. Bake in a preheated 350 degree F. oven for 55 minutes.

KING YELLOW CAKE

2 cups sugar

1 cup butter

5 whole eggs or 10 egg yolks, well beaten

3 cups flour

2 teaspoons cream of tartar

1 teaspoon baking soda

1 cup milk

1 teaspoon vanilla flavoring

Cream the sugar and butter thoroughly. Add the well beaten eggs. Mix together flour and cream of tartar. Dissolve baking soda in milk. Add flour alternately with milk. Add vanilla.

Pour into a tube pan that has been greased and dusted with flour. Bake 45 to 50 minutes in preheated 375 degree F. oven, Freezes well.

ORANGE PUMPKIN CAKE

1 box yellow cake mix

1 1/4 cups canned pumpkin

2/3 cup orange juice

3 eggs

1/4 cup poppy seeds

Combine all, except poppy seeds, in large bowl; beat on low speed, 30 seconds. Beat medium speed, two minutes; stir in the poppy seeds and mix until completely blended.

Pour into a Bundt pan that has been greased and dusted with flour. Bake in oven preheated to 350 degree F. for 35 to 40 minutes, or until wooden pick comes out clean. Cool 10 minutes. Drizzle with glaze.

GLAZE:

1 1/2 cups sifted powdered sugar
3 tablespoons orange juice

Blend sugar and juice until smooth, drizzle on cooled cake.

HERB BUBBLE RING

1 pkg. frozen rolls

2 tablespoons melted butter

1/2 teaspoon whole thyme

3/4 teaspoon garlic powder

1/2 teaspoon oregano

3/4 teaspoon dill

1/2 teaspoon caraway seeds

Thaw the roll dough until pliable. Slice each roll in half; arrange in a lightly

sprayed ring mold or tube pan. Stir together the melted butter and all herbs; brush

over dough. Let dough rise until it has doubled in size. Bake in a preheated 375 degrees F. oven for 25 to 30 minutes, or until brown. Remove bread from the tube pan immediately. Serve hot. Great with pasta or roasts. Easy!

KAILUA CAKE

1 box cake mix, yellow

1 pkg. instant chocolate pudding, 4 serving size

1 cup vegetable oil

1 cup milk

1/4 cup vodka

2 teaspoons cinnamon

1/4 cup Kailua

4 eggs

Combine all the above ingredients, blend for one minute with hand-held mixer on a low speed setting; beat on high speed for two minutes. Spoon into Bundt pan that has been greased and dusted with flour. Bake in a preheated 350 degree F. oven for 45 minutes. Cool for 10 minutes in pan then turn out. Ice the cake with chocolate frosting.

Best Chocolate Frosting:

1/4 cup chocolate chips, semisweet
1/4 cup chocolate, dark
3 tablespoons soft butter
1 tablespoon corn syrup
1/4 teaspoon vanilla extract

Combine all the above in a pan that is over a pan of very (not boiling) hot water. Stir constantly until chocolate melts and all ingredients is well blended. Drizzle over Bundt cake.

LEMON LIME CAKE

1 1/2 cups margarine

3 cups granulated sugar

5 eggs, large

3 cups flour

7 ounces 7-Up

3 cups flour
1 teaspoon lemon flavoring

Cream together the margarine and sugar. Add each egg one egg at a time. Add the remaining ingredients and mix on medium speed until creamy. To give a crust to the outside of the cake, grease the tube pan with butter and sprinkle with powdered sugar before pouring the mixture into the tube pan. Bake in a preheated 350 degree F. oven for 1 hour and 15 minutes. Insert toothpick for doneness test.

RICOTTA CAKE

1 box yellow cake mix

1 pint ricotta cheese

1 egg

1/2 cup sugar

1 teaspoon vanilla

1 jigger Amaretto

Follow cake mix directions and pour into a tube pan that has been greased and dusted with flour. Mix ricotta, egg, sugar, and vanilla together and Amaretto. Spoon mixture over cake batter. Bake in a preheated 350 degree F. oven for 1 hour. Remove from pan after cake is cool. Sprinkle with powdered sugar and a little lemon peel.

Topping:

Powdered sugar
Lemon peel

HOLY COW CAKE

1 box devil's food cake mix

1 1/2 cups water

1/2 cup vegetable oil

3 large eggs

Grease a Bundt pan then dust with flour. In large bowl, mix cake mix, water, oil, and eggs. Beat with electric mixer until smooth. Pour into pan and smooth with spatula. Bake in a preheated 375 degree F oven for 35 minutes. Insert toothpick to check for doneness. Remove pan from oven and place on wire rack. Poke several holes in cake with a straw or toothpick.

Topping:

8 ounces caramel topping
14 ounces sweetened condensed milk
4 Butterfinger candy bars, crushed
12 ounces whipped cream
8 ounces cream cheese

Mix together caramel and condensed milk in a bowl and then pour over cake. Sprinkle half of crushed candy over cake. Place whipped cream and cream cheese in a bowl and blend with electric mixer until well blended and smooth. Spread over cake. Sprinkle the rest of the Butterfinger over the top. Place uncovered in the refrigerator to chill for at least 20 minutes. Store covered in the refrigerator for up to one week.

PECAN CARROT CAKE

2 cups sugar

4 beaten eggs

2 cups cooked carrots, shredded

1/2 teaspoon salt

3 cups flour

1/2 cup pecans, chopped

1 1/2 cups oil

2 teaspoons baking soda

3/4 teaspoon cream of tartar

2 teaspoons cinnamon

2 teaspoons baking powder

Mix all ingredients together and bake inside ungreased tube pan for 1 hour in a preheated 350 degrees F. oven.

SIMPLE BUTTER CAKE

1 cup butter

1 3/4 cup sugar

5 eggs

2 cups flour

1 teaspoon vanilla flavoring

Cream sugar and butter until fluffy and light. Beat each egg one at a time for three minutes each; add to the sugar/butter mixture. Add flour and vanilla. Bake inside a greased angel food cake pan in a preheated 350 degrees F. oven for 1 hour.

FEATHER SPONGE CAKE

8 eggs, separated

1/2 cup water, cold

1 1/2 cups granulated sugar

1 teaspoon vanilla flavoring

1 1/2 cups flour

1/2 teaspoon salt

3/4 teaspoon cream of tartar

Beat egg yolks until thick; add water, sugar and vanilla. Gently fold in flour and salt. In a separate bowl, beat egg whites and cream of tartar until thick. Pour in ungreased tube pan and bake 1 hour at 325 degrees F. Turn upside down to cool about 1 hour.

HOT MILK CAKE

4 eggs

1 teaspoon vanilla flavoring

2 cups granulated sugar

2 teaspoons baking powder

2 cups flour

1 teaspoon salt

1 cup milk

1/2 cup butter, soft

Beat eggs and vanilla; add sugar until thick. Sift baking powder, flour and salt. Add gradually to egg mixture. Heat milk and butter until butter is melted, being careful not to let milk boil. Add milk and butter to batter quickly and stir only to mix.

Pour into a tube pan that has been greased and dusted with flour. Bake in a preheated 350 degrees F. oven for 40 to 45 minutes. Take out of oven and turn upside down on a plate to cool.

SUNSHINE CAKE

12 large eggs, separated

1 teaspoon salt

1 tablespoon lemon juice

1 cup sugar

1 cup cake flour

1 teaspoon cream of tartar

Beat egg whites until stiff and peaks form. Set aside. In another bowl, beat egg yolks until frothy; add salt, lemon juice and sugar and beat well to blend. Pour the egg yolk mixture into the stiffly beaten egg whites, fold lightly. Sift cake flour and cream of tartar three times and sift from sifter into mixture, stirring lightly to blend. Bake in an ungreased tube pan 45 minutes in a preheated 350 degree F. oven.

FROSTING:

3/4 cup softened butter
Powdered sugar
1 egg
1 1/2 cups walnuts, chopped
1 teaspoon vanilla

Combine butter and egg until well mixed. Add vanilla and mix. Beat in enough powdered sugar to make a stiff but pliable paste. Spread over cooled cake and sprinkle liberally with chopped walnuts, if desired.

THE WATERMELON CAKE

1/2 cup butter, soft

3/4 cup sugar

1/2 teaspoon baking soda

1 3/4 cups flour

1/2 teaspoon salt

1 teaspoon cream of tartar

3/4 cup milk

1/2 teaspoon lemon juice

3 egg whites, stiffly beaten

1/2 teaspoon red coloring

1/2 cup raisins

1/2 teaspoon green coloring

1 can white icing

Place sugar and softened butter in bowl and cream together. Sift baking soda, flour, salt and cream of tartar together. Add the flour mixture to sugar and butter mixture alternating with the 3/4 cup milk. Add lemon juice. Fold in egg whites. Take 3/4 of mixture and add red coloring and raisins. Put pink mixture in bottom of tube pan that has been greased and dusted with flour, and then add remaining uncolored cake mixture on top. Bake in a preheated 350 degree F. oven for 50-60 minutes. Frost with white icing with green food coloring added.

ZUCCHINI BUNDT CAKE

1 box spice cake mix

1 cup water

3 eggs

2 tablespoons vegetable oil

1 medium sized zucchini, thinly shredded

1/4 cup walnuts, chopped

3/4 teaspoon vanilla extract

On a baking sheet, spread out the chopped walnuts and let them roast for 6 to 8 minutes in a preheated 350 degree F. oven, stir frequently. Combine in a large bowl the cake mix, oil, eggs (one at a time) and water, follow cake mix directions for mixing. Now add the roasted walnuts, vanilla and zucchini, mix well. Pour batter into a Bundt pan that has been greased and dusted with flour. Bake in a 350 degree F. preheated oven for 40 to 45 minutes. Let cake cool in pan for 10 minutes then place on wire rack or serving plate.

Glaze:

2 teaspoons milk
1/4 cup powdered sugar
1 teaspoon vanilla

Place all of the above ingredients in a small mixing bowl and blend together, drizzle over cake.

MARVELOUS MARBLE CAKE

1/2 cup butter

2 cups sugar

1/2 cup oil

4 eggs, extra large

3 cups flour

1/2 cup nondairy creamer

1/2 cup milk

1 1/2 teaspoons baking powder

2 teaspoons vanilla flavoring

1/4 teaspoon salt

1/4 cup cocoa

Grease a Bundt pan then dust with flour. Place butter, sugar and oil into a large mixing bowl and beat at low speed until well blended. Once blended, beat mixture on high speed until fluffy and light. Add the remaining ingredients, except the cocoa, to the batter and beat at a low speed while constantly scraping. Beat 4 minutes longer on high speed, occasionally scraping. Set aside 2 1/2 cups of batter then pour the remaining batter into pan.

Add the cocoa to the 2 1/2 cups of remaining cake batter and stir. Pour chocolate batter on top of batter in Bundt pan and using a spatula cut the 2 batters together to create the look of marble. Bake for 1 hour in a preheated 350 degree F.

oven. Insert a toothpick into cake for doneness test. Cool cake in pan on a wire rack for approximately 10 minutes.

ZESTY LIME CAKE

3 cups flour

2 teaspoons baking powder

1/2 teaspoon salt

1 cup unsalted butter, softened

2 cups sugar

5 eggs, large

1 cup milk

2 tablespoons lime juice

Zest of 3 limes, finely grated

Grease a Bundt pan then dust with flour. Sift together the baking powder, salt and flour, set aside. Place the unsalted butter and sugar into a large bowl and beat until light and fluffy in texture, then add the eggs. Add alternating portions of dry ingredients and milk to the butter and sugar mixture and blend well. Stir in zest of lime and lime juice. Pour batter into Bundt pan. Bake in a preheated 350 degree F. oven for 1 hour. Let cake cool before turning out.

SIMPLE SOUTHERN CAKE

4 eggs

1 box yellow cake mix, deluxe

12 ounces sour cream

1 container coconut pecan frosting mix

1/4 cup butter, melted

In a large bowl, mix together eggs, cake mix and sour cream. In another bowl, mix together frosting mix and melted butter, stir into cake batter. Pour into a Bundt pan that has been greased and dusted with flour. Bake in a preheated 350 degree F. oven for 50 to 60 minutes.

SO EASY DREAMSICLE CAKE

1 box cake mix, orange supreme

1 box orange flavored gelatin

In a large mixing bowl, mix cake according to the directions on the box and mix in orange gelatin. Cake batter should be light and airy. Bake in a Bundt pan that has been greased and dusted with flour. Cake should cool completely before turning out. Kids love this one!

Icing:

1 cup cool whip, extra creamy
1 container cream cheese frosting
1 can mandarin orange segments, 8 oz.

Drain and crush mandarin orange segments. Mix all ingredients on low speed for 2 minutes. Frost cooled cake.

Holiday Cakes

HOLIDAY CAKES

MOIST APPLE RING CAKE

1 can apple pie filling

1 box spice cake mix

2 eggs

2 tablespoons vegetable oil

1/2 cup chopped pecans

In a blender, blend pie filling till smooth. In a large bowl, combine blended pie filling, cake mix, the eggs and oil. Mix well. Stir in the nuts. Pour into Bundt cake pan that has been greased and dusted with flour. Bake in a preheated 350 degrees F. oven for 50 minutes. (Or until cake springs back when lightly touched.)

Glaze:

2 cups powdered sugar
2 tablespoons water or lemon juice
1/2 teaspoon vanilla

Combine ingredients to make glaze and pour over cooled cake.

EASY EGGNOG POUND CAKE

2 tablespoons butter, softened

1/2 cup almonds, sliced

1 box yellow cake mix

1 1/2 cups eggnog

2 eggs, large

1/4 cup butter, melted

1/8 teaspoons nutmeg

1/4 teaspoon rum flavoring

Generously coat Bundt pan with 2 tablespoons of butter. Spread almonds over the bottom and sides of the buttered Bundt pan. Mix together the cake mix, eggnog, eggs, melted butter, nutmeg and rum flavoring, on medium speed for 4 minutes until batter is completely blended.

Pour batter into Bundt pan and bake inside a preheated 350 degree F. oven for 45 to 50 minutes. Inserted toothpick should come out clean. Cake should cool for ten minutes and then inverted on to a cooling rack. Serve with vanilla ice cream if desired.

ORANGE PASSOVER NUT CAKE

8 eggs, separated

1 1/2 cups sugar

1/2 teaspoon salt

2 teaspoons orange rind, grated

2/3 cup orange juice

1/2 cup walnuts

1 1/4 cups cake meal

Beat egg yolks; add sugar and salt. Add orange rind and juice; beat hard for 3 minutes. Add nuts; mix. Blend cake meal into mixture; fold into stiffly beaten egg whites. Bake in a greased tube pan for 1 hour. Invert cake when done; top with Orange Sauce below.

Orange Sauce:

1/3 cup sugar
1/4 teaspoon salt
1 teaspoon potato starch
1/2 teaspoon orange rind
1 cup orange juice

In saucepan, blend first 3 ingredients. Add rinds; stir juice into mixture gradually. Cook over low heat till it thickens.

MINCEMEAT CAKE

2 cups sugar

1 cup oil

3 eggs

2 cups flour

1/4 teaspoon nutmeg

1 teaspoon baking soda

1 cup buttermilk

1 teaspoon butter or vanilla flavor

1 cup mincemeat

1 cup nuts

Beat together sugar, oil, and eggs for 5 minutes. Sift together flour and nutmeg. Combine the baking soda, buttermilk, and flavoring. Add alternately to sugar, oil, and egg mixture. Stir in mincemeat and nuts. Bake in greased tube pan 1 hour and 15 minutes in a preheated 325 degrees F. oven. Let cake cool completely before turning out.

Glaze:

2 tablespoons melted margarine
1 cup powdered sugar
Juice of 2 lemons

Mix together all of the above and drizzle on top of cooled cake.

RUM AND PECAN CAKE

1 box cake mix, yellow

1 cup pecans or walnuts, chopped

1 box vanilla pudding, instant

1/2 cup rum

4 eggs, large

1/2 cup vegetable oil

1/2 cup water, cold

Mix all the above ingredients (except for nuts) in a large bowl until well blended. Sprinkle chopped nuts into the bottom of a Bundt pan that has been greased and dusted with flour, and then pour in the cake batter. Bake in a preheated 325 degree F. oven for 1 hour.

Glaze:

1/2 cup butter
1/4 cup water
1 cup sugar
1/2 cup rum

Start by melting the butter in a saucepan over low heat. Stir in water and sugar. Boil for five minutes, constantly stirring. Remove saucepan from heat; stir in the 1/2 cup of rum.

Pour over cool cake.

CHRISTMAS CAKE

1 box raisins, 15 oz.

1 box currants, 16 oz.

1 cup walnuts, chopped

1 cup brandy

1 cup butter

1 cup sugar

1 cup flour

6 eggs, separated

Soak first 4 ingredients overnight in a large covered bowl. Cream together the butter and sugar and add egg yolks. Sprinkle flour (about 1/4 cup) on marinated fruit to coat. Fold fruit into butter/sugar mixture. Fold rest of flour into mixture. Beat the egg whites until they are stiff, (not dry) and fold into mixture.

Pour into a tube pan that has been greased and dusted with flour. Bake in a preheated 350 degrees F. oven for 1 hr. Cool and wrap in wax paper. Store in tin for 7-10 days before cutting.

THANKSGIVING PUMPKIN CAKE

1 box yellow cake mix

1/2 cup salad oil

3/4 cup sugar

1 cup pumpkin

1 teaspoon cinnamon

4 eggs, large

1/4 cup water

Dash of nutmeg

Combine all ingredients in a large mixing bowl. Beat 5 minutes with electric mixer. Pour into a tube pan that's been greased and dusted with flour. Bake in a preheated 350 degrees F. oven about 35 minutes or until done. Frost with the Cream Cheese Icing below.

Cream Cheese Icing:

8 ounces cream cheese
1/2 cup margarine, melted
1 box powdered sugar
1 teaspoon vanilla flavoring

Cream margarine and cheese. Add vanilla flavoring and sugar. Beat until smooth.

SPICE AND PUMPKIN CAKE

1 can 100% pumpkin, 15 oz.

1 box spice cake mix

1/2 cup of lukewarm water

In large bowl mix together all the ingredients. Batter will be rather thick. Spread the batter out evenly into a Bundt pan that has been greased and dusted with flour. Bake in a preheated 375 degree F. oven for 40-60 minutes.

CHRISTMAS CANDY CAKE

1 box white cake mix

1/4 cup oil

1 cup water

3 eggs, whites only

1/2 teaspoon peppermint extract

1/2 teaspoon food coloring, red

1/2 cup crushed peppermint hard candy

In a large bowl, beat together white cake mix, oil, water and egg whites using an electric hand mixer on low speed, scraping bowl constantly, until well blended. Continue beating and scrapping the bowl for 2 minutes.

Pour 2 cups of the cake batter into a Bundt pan that's been greased and dusted with flour. Pour approximately 3/4 cup of cake batter into a bowl and stir in peppermint extract and red food coloring.

Pour peppermint batter over the batter in the pan, top with remaining white batter, pouring slowly. Bake in a preheated 350 degree F. oven for 45 to 50 minutes. Cake should pull away from sides of pan when done. Let cake cool for 1 hour. Top with white icing and crushed peppermint candy.

RUM EGGNOG BUNDT CAKE

1/2 cup butter, softened

1 cup eggnog

3 eggs, large

1/4 cup rum

1 box white cake mix

1 teaspoon nutmeg

2 teaspoons vanilla

In a mixing bowl, add butter and beat until fluffy and light, then beat in eggnog, eggs and rum. Add the cake mix, nutmeg and vanilla; beat on slow until well blended, beat on high for 2 more minutes. Grease a Bundt pan then dust with flour and spoon in the batter. Bake in a preheated 325 degree F. oven for 35 to 45 minutes. Insert toothpick for doneness test.

YUMMY RUM CAKE

1 cup butter, softened
1 1/2 cups sugar
1 1/2 cups flour
1/4 teaspoon baking powder
1/8 teaspoon salt
4 eggs, separated
1 teaspoon vanilla
1 teaspoon almond extract
2 ounces rum
1/2 cup pecans, chopped

Cream butter. Gradually add sugar. Add flour, baking powder, salt and egg yolks, one at a time. Add liquids. Beat whites stiff and fold in. Grease and line the bottom of a tube pan with waxed paper. Cover bottom of pan with one-half cup chopped pecans.

Pour cake mixture into pan and bake in a preheated 350 degrees F. oven for ten minutes; then at 300 degrees F. for one hour.

KAILUA CAKE

1 box cake mix, yellow

1/4 cup sugar

1 pkg. chocolate pudding, instant

1 cup oil

4 eggs

2/3 cup water

1/4 cup vodka

1/4 cup Kailua

Using a large mixing bowl, mix together all of the ingredients. Pour into a Bundt pan that has been greased and dusted with flour. Bake in a 350 degree F. preheated oven for 50 to 60 minutes, or until cake springs back. Cool 10 minutes. Turn pan over on plate. Poke holes in cake with fork and pour glaze over cake.

Glaze:

1/4 cup Kailua
1/2 cup powdered sugar

Blend together the two ingredients and drizzle over cake.

BREAKFAST BUNDT CAKE

2 cans Grands biscuits

6 eggs, beaten

3 cups sharp cheddar cheese, shredded

1 pound of breakfast sausage, cooked and drained

Coat a Bundt with grease and dust with flour. Place a layer of one can of Grand's biscuits on the bottom of the Bundt pan; be sure to overlap them slightly. Top biscuits with breakfast sausage, eggs, and sharp cheddar cheese. Place remaining biscuits on top, and again be sure to overlap them slightly. Place in a preheated 350 degree F. oven for 10 to 15 minutes. Run a knife around the edges and turn out on a serving plate. Serve with fresh fruit if desired.

MEXICAN BREAKFAST BUNDT

1 pound cooked sausage, extra sage

1/2 pound bacon, fully cook and crumbled

9 eggs

2 cups pepper jack cheese

1 can biscuits, cut into quarters

1 small can green chilies, chopped

1/4 cup chunky salsa

1/2 cup onion, finely diced

1/4 cup jalapenos, chopped (optional)

Lightly grease a Bundt pan. In a large bowl, mix together sausage, bacon, onion, jalapenos and biscuits. Add remainder of the ingredients and mix well.

Pour mixture into Bundt pan. Bake in a preheated 350 degree F. oven for 30 minutes. Let cool for 5 minutes, loosen edges with knife and turn out on a serving plate. Serve warm.

Photo credits:

Cover photo by James Loftus / Photos.com

Other photos:

Robert Linton

Dmytro Mykhailov

Studioraffi

Manyakotic

Jill Chen

SoleilC

Other books by Tera L. Davis

Tex-Mex Recipes - 100 Recipes to Spice Up Your Appetite

Available at Amazon.com in Kindle and Paperback Editions

Made in the USA
Lexington, KY
25 August 2015